Creepy Creatures

Bees

Sue Barraclough

Heinemann
LIBRARY

Little Nippers

www.heinemann.co.uk/library
Visit our website to find out more information about **Heinemann Library** books.

To order:
☎ Phone 44 (0) 1865 888066
▤ Send a fax to 44 (0) 1865 314091
▣ Visit the Heinemann Bookshop at www.heinemann.co.uk/library to browse our catalogue and order online.

First published in Great Britain by Heinemann Library, Halley Court, Jordan Hill, Oxford OX2 8EJ, part of Harcourt Education.
Heinemann is a registered trademark of Harcourt Education Ltd.

Editorial: Sarah Shannon and Louise Galpine
Design: Jo Hinton-Malivoire and bigtop, Bicester UK
Picture Research: Hannah Taylor and Sally Claxton
Production: Camilla Smith

Originated by Dot Gradations
Printed and bound in China by South China Printing Company

ISBN 0 431 93257 3 (hardback)
09 08 07 06 05
10 9 8 7 6 5 4 3 2 1

ISBN 0 431 93262 X (paperback)
09 08 07 06 05
10 9 8 7 6 5 4 3 2 1

British Library Cataloguing in Publication Data
Barraclough, Sue
595.7'99
Creepy Creatures: Bees
A full catalogue record for this book is available from the British Library.

Acknowledgements
The publishers would like to thank the following for permission to reproduce photographs: Alamy Images pp. 12, 21 (archivberlin Fotoagentur GmbH), 13 (Chris Howes/ Wild Places Photography), 22-23 (Comstock Images), 11 (Grady Harrison), 19 (Wildchromes), 14 (Worldwide Picture Library); Ardea 7 top, (J L Mason), 16 (John Mason); Corbis pp. 6, 15 (Treat Davidson; Frank Lane Picture Agency), 18 (George D. Lepp), 4 (Michael Maconachie; Papilio); FLPA p.20 (Treat Davidson); Garden Matters p.10 (Debbie Wager Stock Pics); Getty Images pp.7 bottom, 8, 9 (Photodisc); Holt Studios International Ltd pp. 5, 17.

Cover photograph of a bee, reproduced with permission of Getty Images/ Taxi.

Contents

Bees 4

Different bees 6

Looking for bees 8

A bee's body 10

Buzzing bees 12

A bee's home 14

Bees' eggs 16

Food for bees 18

Bees in danger 20

Bees in winter 22

Index 24

Bees

Bees are *small* buzzing insects.

They often have yellow and brown stripy bodies.

Different bees

There are many different types of bee.

Bees can be different sizes and shapes.

Looking for bees

You might see bees in parks, gardens, and woods.

Can you can see them flying from flower to flower?

9

A bee's body

Bees are insects. They have three parts to their bodies.

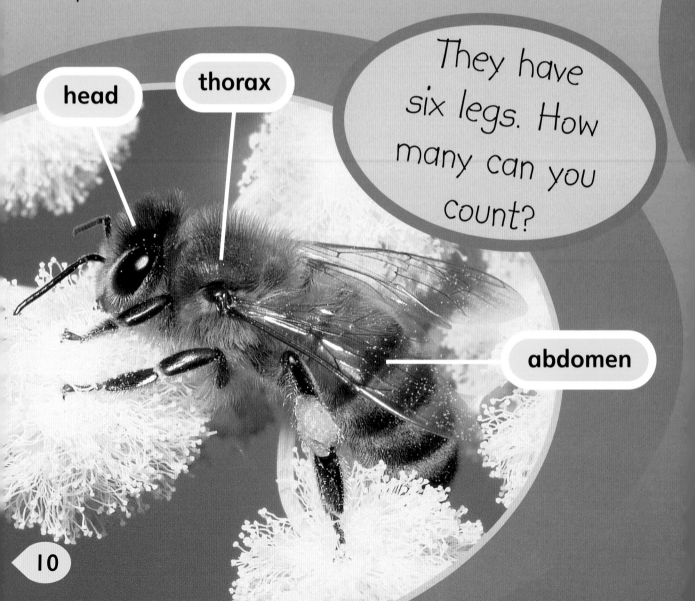

head

thorax

They have six legs. How many can you count?

abdomen

Bees have two antennae for tasting, touching, and even hearing.

Buzzing bees

A bee has two pairs of thin, see-through wings.

The wings move so fast that they make a buzzing sound.

Buzzzzzzzz...

A bee's home

Most bees live in
big groups called colonies.
Each bee has a job
to do.

A queen bee is much
bigger than the other
bees. Her job is
to lay eggs.

15

Bees' eggs

larvae

The eggs change and grow into larvae. Worker bees look after the eggs.

Some work to keep
the eggs clean.
Others find food
for the young.

Food for bees

Bees suck up nectar from flowers. They collect pollen on their **hairy** back legs.

pollen

Bees have a very **long**, tube-like tongue for sucking up nectar.

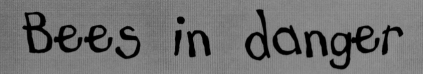

Bees in danger

Not many animals eat bees because they have a painful sting.

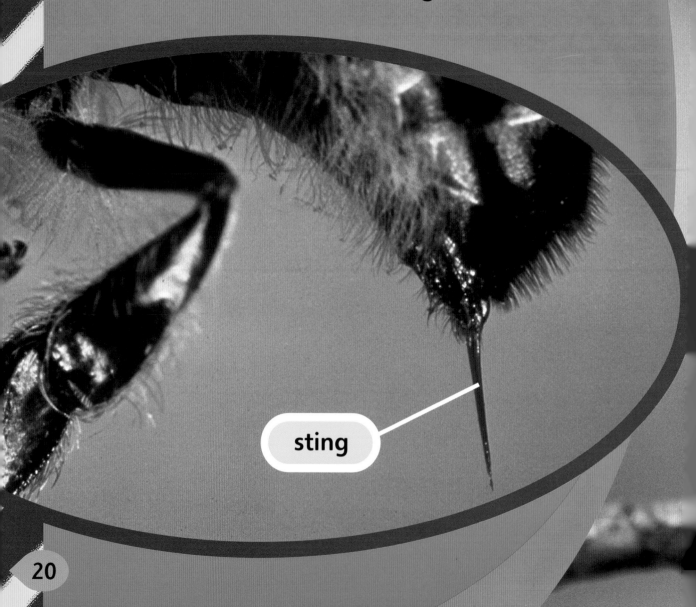

sting

A bee-eater is a bird that will eat bees and other insects.

21

Bees in winter

honey

In cold weather the bees stay in the nest and eat their store of honey.

Index

antennae.......... 11

colony........... 14

egg 16, 17

larvae 16, 17

nectar 18, 19

pollen 18, 19

queen bee 15

sting 20, 21

wing 12, 13

Notes for adults

This series supports the young child's exploration of their learning environment and their knowledge and understanding of their world. The four books when used together will enable comparison of similarities and differences to be made. (N.B. Many of the photographs in **Creepy Creatures** show the creatures much larger than life size. The first spread of each title shows the creature at approximately its real life size.)

The following Early Learning Goals are relevant to the series:
• Find out about, and identify, some features of living things, objects, and events that they observe
• Ask questions about why things happen and how things work
• Observe, find out about, and identify features in the place they live and the natural world
• Find out about their local environment and talk about those features they like and dislike.

The books will help the child extend their vocabulary, as they will hear new words. Since words are used in context in the book this should enable the young child to gradually incorporate them into their own vocabulary. Some of the words that may be new to them in **Bees** are *thorax, abdomen, antennae, colonies, larvae, nectar,* and *pollen.*

The following additional information may be of interest:

Bees are social insects, so they live in large, well-organized groups. Most honeybees live in man-made hives, but before they were domesticated honeybees made their nests in hollow trees in woodlands. The hives need to be close to good food supplies of pollen and nectar. Bees build a structure inside the hive called a honeycomb. It is made of wax that the worker bees produce. They chew and mould the wax to form the individual cells. The cells are then used to store food and also act as nurseries for the young. The queen bee usually lays her eggs between March and October. Bees carry out a vital role in pollination of flowering plants, because they carry pollen from flower to flower as they fly around collecting nectar. Honey is made from regurgitated nectar.

Follow-up activities

Children might like to follow up what they have learned about bees by making their own observations in parks and gardens. Develop ideas and understanding by discussing any features they find interesting, and encourage children to record their ideas and observations in drawings, paintings, or writing.